RENOVATE

TO MAKE NEW

NP

NORTH POINT
RESOURCES

TABLE OF CONTENTS

INTRODUCTION 4

SESSION 1: Check the Foundation 7

SESSION 2: Assess for Damage 17

SESSION 3: Review the Records 31

SESSION 4: Call a Professional 47

SESSION 5: Draw Up the Plan 55

SESSION 6: Demo Day 63

SESSION 7: Take Out the Trash 71

SESSION 8: Hard Hats On 81

APPENDIX 93

LEADER GUIDE 119

INTRODUCTION

Have you ever attempted a renovation? You start off motivated but often end the first day with a massive mess on your hands. We've all been there. So, here's the question: *If renovation is so difficult, why do we attempt it?*

Over the course of eight sessions, this study will introduce you to the possibility of a personal renovation by exploring the foundation and blueprints of God's original design for us.

Remember, renovation is optional—not everyone is up for the challenge. Whether you choose to undergo a complete overhaul or just freshen the paint, we think you'll look back on this renovation process and be amazed by the end result.

Are you ready to renovate?

FLOW OF A RENOVATE SESSION

SOCIALIZE (10 MINUTES)
Spend a few minutes getting to know one another and catching up.

DISCUSS (10 MINUTES – OPTIONAL)
Talk about the homework completed the previous week:

> Was anything helpful to you? If so, what?

> What was more challenging than you expected?

WATCH (15 MINUTES)
The video session enhances the materials in the workbook by providing additional content on the topic.

DISCUSS (45 MINUTES)
The Discussion Questions provided in each session help participants explore the topic in conversation with one another. The questions are designed to allow people the freedom to reveal tensions or struggles with the topic, make personal discoveries, or think more about the subject.

REVIEW THE HOMEWORK (5 MINUTES)
The *Renovate* experience is different for each person. Some people may choose to skip certain exercises, while others will choose to complete all of them. Assure participants that they have the freedom to do as much or as little of the homework as they desire.

PRAY (5 MINUTES)
Sharing prayer requests and praying for one another is an important part of the experience. It is also okay for a participant not to share anything. Pressure should never be applied to disclose prayer requests.

1

Check the Foundation

SESSION 1:
CHECK THE FOUNDATION

When it comes to a personal renovation, we tend to focus on symptoms instead of causes. That's not our fault. We're inundated with self-help books, experts, counselors, and even pastors who offer advice on symptoms instead of root causes. Most of the advice we hear about personal growth focuses on changing problematic behaviors or negative emotions. But the driving force behind how we act and feel is *what we believe.*

If beliefs drive our behaviors and emotions, how do we get rid of problematic behaviors and emotions? We change the beliefs that drive them. Two people raised under the same roof can respond in radically different ways to the same circumstances because they view life through different sets of beliefs.

Some beliefs are true. Others are not. The false beliefs are the ones that cause problems. In order to change the unhealthy behaviors and emotions associated with things like worry or jealousy, we have to substitute the truths for the false beliefs that drive them.

INFLUENCES

We all have beliefs that were influenced by three aspects of our pasts:

> Relationships (*parents, peers*)
>
> Events (*activities, traumas, rejections*)
>
> Church experiences (*no involvement, legalism*)

These influences, as powerful as they were, do not have to dictate how you behave and what you believe. You don't have to keep living with the false beliefs that were ingrained in you from an early age.

EMOTIONS

Just like behaviors, emotions have beliefs behind them. We live in a culture that tells us to allow our emotions to drive our behaviors.

> *"If it feels good, do it."*

> *"I went with my gut."*

> *"It didn't feel right, so I didn't do it."*

What's wrong with this philosophy?

1. Emotions can and will deceive you.

2. Emotions don't distinguish between fiction and reality.

3. Sometimes following God requires setting aside your emotions, ignoring your "gut," and stepping out in faith.

CONCLUSION

Many of the beliefs you carry today were formed during childhood. You have the option to evaluate them, determining where they came from and whether they are true or false. The first step to your renovation is checking the foundation to determine the areas of your life that need overhauls.

VIDEO NOTES

SESSION 1 COMMUNICATOR: CHRIS KIM

Chris has been with North Point Ministries for seven years. He is the Starting Point Director and the Director of Community Groups at Woodstock City Church. He provides leadership for a Groups staff that supports volunteers leading Men's, Women's, Married, and Starting Point groups. Chris and his wife, Debbie, have one daughter.

IN-SESSION ACTIVITY

Any renovation begins with a thorough assessment of the room or home you wish to renovate. Similarly, you can't move forward until you understand where you are and what has influenced the way you think.

Below is a list of phrases that describe various influences. Check the boxes that are true for you.

INFLUENTIAL RELATIONSHIPS

- ☐ Family member who bullied
- ☐ Family member who shamed
- ☐ Family member with addiction
- ☐ Family member with mental illness
- ☐ Parent who acted like a child
- ☐ Parent who celebrated achievement
- ☐ Parent who denied feelings ("Don't feel that way.")
- ☐ Parent who disciplined inconsistently
- ☐ Parent who disregarded achievement
- ☐ Parent who praised inconsistently
- ☐ Parent who expected child to act like a parent
- ☐ Parent who focused on appearances
- ☐ Parent who gave child excessive praise

- ☐ Parent who minimized problems
- ☐ Parent who over-disciplined
- ☐ Parent who was absent (emotionally or physically)
- ☐ Parent who was dependent
- ☐ Parent who was over-controlling
- ☐ Parent who was over-indulgent
- ☐ Parent who was over-protective
- ☐ Parent with excessive standards
- ☐ Peer rejection
- ☐ Peers who bullied
- ☐ Peers who focused on appearances
- ☐ Peers who were competitive
- ☐ Peers who were critical

Are any influential relationships from your life not listed above? If so, what are they?

INFLUENTIAL EVENTS

☐ A breakup

☐ A parent's affair

☐ Abandoned by parent

☐ Basic needs not met

☐ Divorce of parents

☐ Death of a parent

☐ Death of a sibling

☐ Death of a friend

☐ Emotional abuse

☐ Life-threatening illness

☐ Moved often

☐ Natural disaster

☐ Neglected

☐ Observed abuse of a parent

☐ Physical abuse

☐ Sexual abuse

☐ Verbal abuse

Are any influential events from your life not listed above? If so, what are they?

INFLUENTIAL CHURCH EXPERIENCES

☐ Attended church regularly

☐ Church scandal

☐ Church split

☐ Confirmation or baptism

☐ Female-led church

☐ Highly conservative

☐ Highly liberal

☐ Hypocritical

☐ Legalistic

☐ Male-led church

☐ No faith or church involvement

☐ Parents of two different faiths

☐ Religious abuse (oppression)

☐ Shaming

☐ Works-based religion

Are any influential religious experiences from your life not listed above? If so, what are they?

Once you have completed the activity, begin the *Discussion Questions*.

DISCUSSION QUESTIONS

1. Were you reserved or outgoing as a child? To what extent has that tendency continued into your adulthood?

_____

_____

2. Talk about a time you changed a behavior in order to achieve a specific goal. Did you achieve your goal? Was the change in behavior lasting?

_____

_____

3. Talk about an influential relationship, event, or church experience that came to mind as you worked through the _In-Session Activity_. Was that influence positive or negative?

_____

_____

4. In what ways has that influential relationship, event, or church experience shaped what you believe and how you behave?

_____

_____

5. In the video message, Chris says, "To change our unhealthy behaviors, we have to change our false beliefs." Is that difficult for you to believe? Why or why not?

_____

_____

PRIMER:
THE HOMEWORK FOR THIS WEEK
☐ Complete the *Identifying False Beliefs* exercise, pp. 15–16. (10 minutes)
☐ Read Session 2, pp. 18–19. (5 minutes)

SECOND COAT:
IF YOU WANT MORE
☐ After completing the *Identifying False Beliefs* exercise, spend some additional time reading your answers and thinking about the content from this session.

HOMEWORK:
IDENTIFYING FALSE BELIEFS

Check each of the following false beliefs you identify with or you tell yourself.

☐ 1. I must be in control to be safe, secure, or significant.

☐ 2. I must please other people to be loved or accepted.

☐ 3. I must overcome and make it; I must be tough and independent to survive.

☐ 4. To be safe and secure, I must be guarded and not risk intimacy.

☐ 5. Emotions always represent truth.

☐ 6. For me to be content, life must be fair.

☐ 7. I am unworthy of love or acceptance.

☐ 8. I must be right to be significant or to know I am of value.

☐ 9. I must be heard to know I am of value.

☐ 10. I cannot be okay or at peace if those around me are not okay.

☐ 11. I deserve special treatment from other people.

☐ 12. I must have respect to know I am of value.

☐ 13. I must perform/achieve to be accepted.

☐ 14. What I do makes me who I am.

☐ 15. My loved ones must change for me to be content and at peace.

☐ 16. Other people must meet my needs.

☐ 17. I must get revenge on those who have wronged me.

☐ 18. I must be protected to know I am safe and secure.

☐ 19. I must have the approval of other people to know I am of value. Their opinions of me determine my worth.

☐ 20. I must be in a relationship or married to be satisfied, secure, or significant.

☐ 21. If I follow the Lord, life will be hard.

☐ 22. I am a victim.

☐ 23. My past determines who I am.

☐ 24. I must meet certain standards to love, accept, and feel good about myself.

☐ 25. I must have a child to fill my emptiness.

☐ 26. I must figure out my future to be secure.

☐ 27. I can't handle this.

Material adapted from *Old Beliefs vs New Beliefs* by Anne Trippe. Used with permission.

☐ 28. I must be appreciated to know I am of value.

☐ 29. I do not measure up.

☐ 30. I'm worthless. I will never amount to anything.

☐ 31. I am responsible for the happiness of other people, and they are responsible for mine.

☐ 32. I must fix problems to know I am secure.

☐ 33. In order to feel worthy, I must not fail.

☐ 34. I must be the best to know that I am of value.

☐ 35. I must get my way to be satisfied and content.

☐ 36. I must earn love.

☐ 37. Real men do not show they need help.

☐ 38. I cannot be happy unless my circumstances change.

☐ 39. I must be understood to have peace and contentment.

☐ 40. I cannot allow other people to see my flaws. I must be perfect to know I am of value and to be secure.

☐ 41. The shame of my past is my fault, and I am to blame for the consequences of it.

☐ 42. I am who I am. I shouldn't have to change.

☐ 43. I deserve what I have. I worked hard for it.

☐ 44. I must prove myself to know my worth.

☐ 45. I must take care of myself.

☐ 46. Others cannot be trusted.

☐ 47. I must protect my reputation to feel valued.

Do you have a false belief that is not listed above? If so, write it out here.

_____

_____

Our false beliefs influence our behaviors and emotions and can ultimately affect our relationship with God. Over the next few weeks, we will explore the correlation between your false beliefs and behaviors and see how God is able to transform you.

2

Assess for Damage

SESSION 2:
ASSESS FOR DAMAGE

It may sound strange to us that the apostle Paul wrote about living in our "flesh." What is that all about? Paul was referring to the antagonist that lives inside us that wants its own way—even when its own way is unhealthy. Galatians 5:16 says, "So I say, walk by the Spirit, and you will not gratify the desires of the flesh."

Our flesh isn't who we are—it's how we behave and respond emotionally when we don't walk in the Spirit. Your flesh may tell you that you're a disaster of a human being, or it may convince you that you're self-sufficient and have no need for God. Obeying the desires of the flesh makes you feel distant from God.

OVERCOMING THE FLESH

Our flesh is all about trying to meet our needs on our own, apart from God. Since our behaviors and emotions are driven by beliefs, our unhealthy behaviors and emotions are helpful in identifying ways we live out our lives apart from Christ.

As you begin to work through what it means to live in the flesh, you'll probably wonder, *If my flesh is not really who I am, then who am I?* This is normal. You'll need to spend time wrestling with this. It may be especially confusing if the way you live in the flesh is socially acceptable.

THE THREE NEEDS

There's nothing inherently wrong with needs. God created us with needs. They fall into three broad categories:

Security (*Safety*)

Satisfaction (*Happiness*)

Significance (*Value*)

What matters is how you go about meeting those needs. It defines who you are. That's because the choices we make as we pursue security, satisfaction, and significance become the ways we shape our identities. They tell us who we are or who we want to be. Do you find security in money or material possessions? Do you find satisfaction in carrying the title of devoted parent or spouse? Do you find significance in your career?

Or do you look to God for security, satisfaction, and significance?

CONCLUSION

The sense of independence we all crave is not inherently good or bad. You can be independent in the flesh, working to meet your needs, or you can be independent as a result of God living through you. The way you go about getting this independence makes all the difference. It usually takes time and reflection to figure out if you're trying to meet legitimate needs in the flesh or if you're relying on Christ.

VIDEO NOTES

SESSION 2 COMMUNICATOR: GAVIN ADAMS

Gavin Adams is the lead pastor of Woodstock City Church. Before joining Woodstock City in 2008, Gavin was the Family Ministry Director of Southside Church. Gavin and his wife, Chantel, have been married for 19 years and have four children.

IN-SESSION ACTIVITY

1. Go through the list of common ways we meet needs on our own. Check the boxes in the first column for the things that are important to you.

NOTE: The second part of this exercise can be completed in-session or as homework.

2. Needs are often categorized into three areas:

   Security (Safety)

   Satisfaction (Happiness)

   Significance (Value)

For each box you checked in the first column, categorize how you are trying to meet those needs by asking yourself this question:

Example: *Does _____ have an impact on my _____?*

   *Does **my appearance** have an impact on my **satisfaction**?*

	Important	Security (Safety)	Satisfaction (Happiness)	Significance (Value)
My appearance	☐	☐	☐	☐
My weight	☐	☐	☐	☐
Avoiding conflict with other people	☐	☐	☐	☐
Everything being "fine"	☐	☐	☐	☐
Controlling circumstances	☐	☐	☐	☐
Being emotionally supported	☐	☐	☐	☐
Being financially supported	☐	☐	☐	☐
Having friends	☐	☐	☐	☐
Loyalty of friends	☐	☐	☐	☐

	Important	Security (Safety)	Satisfaction (Happiness)	Significance (Value)
Commitment from others	☐	☐	☐	☐
Having a significant other	☐	☐	☐	☐
The success of my significant other	☐	☐	☐	☐
My financial situation	☐	☐	☐	☐
Follow-through	☐	☐	☐	☐
Material possessions	☐	☐	☐	☐
Approval from others	☐	☐	☐	☐
Positive facial expressions	☐	☐	☐	☐
Protection	☐	☐	☐	☐
A provider	☐	☐	☐	☐
Stability	☐	☐	☐	☐
Validation	☐	☐	☐	☐
Being heard	☐	☐	☐	☐
Appreciation	☐	☐	☐	☐
Encouragement	☐	☐	☐	☐
Recognition	☐	☐	☐	☐
Pleasing others	☐	☐	☐	☐
Food	☐	☐	☐	☐
Alcohol	☐	☐	☐	☐
Drugs	☐	☐	☐	☐
Sex	☐	☐	☐	☐

	Important	Security (Safety)	Satisfaction (Happiness)	Significance (Value)
Being married	☐	☐	☐	☐
Marital fidelity	☐	☐	☐	☐
Emotional stability	☐	☐	☐	☐
Financial stability	☐	☐	☐	☐
Owning a house	☐	☐	☐	☐
A clean house	☐	☐	☐	☐
Having children	☐	☐	☐	☐
Having well-behaved children	☐	☐	☐	☐
Organization and structure	☐	☐	☐	☐
My education	☐	☐	☐	☐
My career	☐	☐	☐	☐
My performance	☐	☐	☐	☐
My competence	☐	☐	☐	☐
Being adequate	☐	☐	☐	☐
Success	☐	☐	☐	☐
Job titles	☐	☐	☐	☐
My achievement	☐	☐	☐	☐
Who I know	☐	☐	☐	☐
My reputation	☐	☐	☐	☐
My emotional health	☐	☐	☐	☐
My physical health	☐	☐	☐	☐

Once you have completed the activity, begin the *Discussion Questions*.

DISCUSSION QUESTIONS

1. Do you consider yourself a thinker or a feeler? How have you benefitted from that tendency? What problems has it caused you?

_____

_____

2. Review your results from the *In-Session Activity*. What did they indicate that you pursue most—security, satisfaction, or significance? Do you agree with your results? Why or why not?

_____

_____

3. In the video, Gavin defines "the flesh" as "a dependency on anything other than Jesus as the ultimate source to meet our needs." Respond to that statement. Does looking to Jesus to meet all of your needs seem reasonable? Why or why not?

_____

_____

4. How do you think the ways of meeting the needs you identified in the *In-Session Activity* are keeping you from growing with God, finding peace, or discovering life to the full?

_____

_____

5. How do you think you might benefit from understanding how your emotions influence the ways you try to meet your needs apart from Jesus?

_____

_____

PRIMER:
THE HOMEWORK FOR THIS WEEK
☐ Complete the *Behaviors and Emotions* exercise, pp. 26–27. (10 minutes)
☐ Complete the *Mapping My Flesh* exercise, pp. 28–29. (20 minutes)
☐ Read Session 3, pp. 32–34. (5 minutes)

SECOND COAT:
IF YOU WANT MORE
☐ Read *Influences: Common By-Products* located in the Appendix, pp. 94–97. It lists common behaviors and emotions that present themselves in the lives of people who have experienced certain relationships or events.

HOMEWORK:
BEHAVIORS AND
EMOTIONS {OF MY FLESH}

Below is a list of words or phrases that describe behaviors and emotions resulting from our flesh. Check the boxes that seem to be present in your life most of the time.

☐ Aggressive

☐ Angry

☐ Anxious (lacking peace)

☐ Argumentative

☐ Arrogant (cocky)

☐ Bitter

☐ Blaming other people

☐ Compulsive

☐ Controlled by doubts

☐ Controlled by emotions

☐ Controlled by other people

☐ Controlling

☐ Critical (negative)

☐ Deceitful (misleading)

☐ Defensive

☐ Depressed

☐ Despairing

☐ Dominant

☐ Emotionally withdrawn

☐ Envious

☐ Exaggerating

☐ Falsely humble

☐ Falsely spiritual

☐ Fearful

☐ Gossipy

☐ Guilt-ridden

☐ Harsh

☐ Hateful

☐ Hold grudges

☐ Impatient

☐ Inadequate

☐ Independent

☐ Inferior

☐ Inflexible

☐ Insecure

☐ Insensitive

☐ Intolerant

☐ Jealous

☐ Judgmental

☐ Lacking in compassion

☐ Lacking in self-control

☐ Lacking in trust (easily suspicious)

☐ Lust for sex

☐ Make excuses

☐ Manipulative

☐ Materialistic

☐ Must please other people

☐ Nervous

☐ Overeat

☐ Passive-aggressive

☐ Perfectionist

☐ Poor listener

☐ Possessive

☐ Power-seeking

☐ Prideful

☐ Rebel against authority

☐ Resentful

☐ Restless

☐ Rude

☐ Sarcastic

☐ Self-condemning

☐ Self-confident

☐ Self-deprecating

☐ Self-indulgent

☐ Self-justifying

☐ Self-pitying

☐ Self-reliant

☐ Self-righteous

☐ Selfishly ambitious

☐ Slanderous

☐ Slow to forgive

☐ Too opinionated

☐ Too quick to speak

☐ Too sensitive to criticism

☐ Too strict

☐ Too subjective

☐ Too submissive

☐ Uncooperative

☐ Undisciplined

☐ Unemotional

☐ Unreasonable

☐ Unreliable

☐ Unsympathetic

☐ Unteachable

HOMEWORK:
MAPPING MY FLESH

Over the last two sessions, we have looked into our pasts to explore the correlation between our influences, false beliefs, behaviors, and emotions. This exercise is designed to help you map out your flesh as well as assist you in determining some patterns that may exist in your life.

INFLUENCES
See pages 11–12 for the influences you selected. Write out your top three in the space provided.

- _____

- _____

- _____

FALSE BELIEFS
See pages 15–16 for the false beliefs you selected. Write out your top three in the space provided.

- _____

- _____

- _____

WALL OF BEHAVIORS AND EMOTIONS

See pages 26–27 for the behaviors and emotions you exhibit. Write the ones you selected in the space provided.

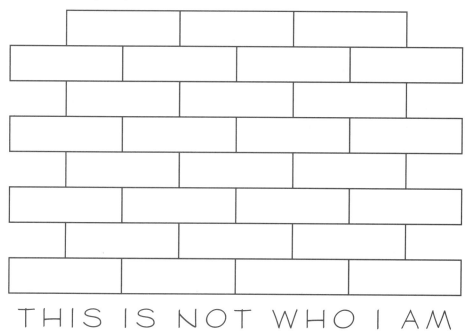

THIS IS NOT WHO I AM

When we are able to map out our flesh patterns, it helps to identify our flesh for what it is: messy, ugly, and not how God designed us to operate. This exercise is often difficult to work through, and you may come to the end of it feeling disappointed or overwhelmed. The good news is that this is not who you really are. Flesh is a dependency on anything other than Jesus as the ultimate source to meet your needs. God designed you for so much more. In the next session, we will look at how you can move away from your unhealthy flesh patterns and toward a discovery of who God says you are.

3

Review the Records

SESSION 3:
REVIEW THE RECORDS

Over the past two sessions, we've been exploring the power of false beliefs and the influences that assist in the construction of those beliefs. In Session 1, we said that you can't simply disregard false beliefs; you have to replace them with new beliefs. In this session, we will talk about how you do that.

The apostle Paul provided clear advice on how to manage the dilemma of false beliefs: "Take every thought captive and make it obedient to Christ" (2 Corinthians 10:5) and "Be transformed by the renewing of your mind" (Romans 12:2).

There is one tool you need to repair a false belief: the truth. Lies fade and disappear when we dispute them with the truth, allowing us to experience new, healthy behaviors and emotions. That's what Paul meant when he wrote about "the renewing of your mind."

Scripture calls us to walk in the truth, love the truth, and believe the truth.

Our culture confuses truth with facts. Truth is factual, but it is more than that. It cannot be changed, but it changes us. It frees us from the false beliefs of the flesh: "Then you will know the truth, and the truth will set you free" (John 8:32).

KNOWING YOUR STORY

Understanding your story matters. That's because many of your beliefs were formed by experiences, both positive and negative, during your childhood. Some of those beliefs aren't true. The first step to replacing those false beliefs with truth—the truth of who God is and who you are in Christ—is to identify them. That requires understanding your story.

You can't chart a course to your future until you understand where you are and where you've been. Being physically, emotionally, and spiritually healthy requires knowing how God designed you to be and to live. Too often, we live contrary to how we were created. We struggle to be something we're not. We allow our personal histories and circumstances to tell us who we are, and then we exhaust ourselves working to be those people. And as you grow in your faith and understanding of your story, you'll be better equipped to interpret your past, which will help you grow even more.

A DISTORTED VIEW OF GOD

We believe that the essence of truth is found in the Bible: truth about who we are, truth about others, and truth about God. Your relationship with your earthly father can impact how you view your heavenly Father. One obstacle to a person understanding and believing truth, particularly truth about God, is a defective view of one's heavenly Father.

If we want to live lives grounded and stabilized by truth, we need to have an accurate view of God. A distorted view of God causes major obstructions because it affects every area of our lives.

Your father may have been one of these common father types:

Absent or Distant:

- Physically: he is not around most of the time and rarely interacts with his child (often due to work, divorce, or death).
- Emotionally: he shows little emotion or affection.

Children of absent or distant fathers often see God as uninvolved or uninterested in their lives.

Abusive:

- He inflicts emotional, physical, verbal, or sexual pain.
- He destroys his child's sense of worth.
- He fosters distrust in his child.

Children of abusive fathers often have difficulty trusting God or relating to him emotionally.

Authoritarian:

- He is concerned with obedience and performance.
- He is uninterested in his child's opinions, ideas, or desires.
- He is intent on his own way.

Children of authoritarian fathers often end up rebelling against God.

Critical or Judgmental:

- He criticizes his children.
- He holds his children to an impossible standard.

Children of critical or judgmental fathers often believe that God will never be pleased with who they are or what they accomplish.

Involved:

- He knows his children well.
- He interacts with his children often.

Children of involved fathers tend to assume that God is loving and cares for them individually.

Regardless of the type of father you had, that relationship likely influenced how you view God. Sometimes, even the best earthly fathers leave us with some false beliefs about God.

CONCLUSION

Whatever your false beliefs about God, your next step is to begin to replace them with the truth. God is the perfect Father. He knows, loves, and disciplines you perfectly. To change the way you think about God, yourself, and others, begin by renewing your mind and reviewing what the Bible says is true.

VIDEO NOTES

SESSION 3 COMMUNICATOR: JOHN WOODALL

John Woodall is the Director of (7) and Men's Groups at North Point Community Church. Previously, John served as a senior pastor in Florida and Virginia. John and his wife, Debbie, have been married for 40 years. They have three sons, one daughter, and eleven grandchildren.

IN-SESSION ACTIVITY

It is important to understand your story. Many of your beliefs were formed by influential experiences and relationships, both positive and negative. Your "story," or your "history," is often a summary of the moments and relationships that influenced you the most.

The following questions are designed to help you think through your story. Consider the things you've wanted—career, family, adventure, spiritual experiences—and the obstacles you've faced while pursuing them.

1. Who are 1–2 people that have greatly influenced me?

_____

_____

_____

2. What is one of my most memorable successes?

_____

_____

_____

3. What obstacles did I overcome to achieve that success?

_____

_____

_____

   Material adapted from *Community: Starting Well*, North Point Resources. Used with permission.

4. What is one of my most memorable failures?

_____

_____

_____

5. What did I learn from that failure?

_____

_____

_____

Once you have completed the activity, begin the *Discussion Questions*.

DISCUSSION QUESTIONS

1. Talk about a time when you learned from failing. Did it change your perspective on failure? If so, how?

_____

_____

2. Is the idea that *your experiences during the first two decades of life have influenced your current behavior* new to you? Do you believe that's true? Why or why not?

_____

_____

3. What kind of relationship did you have with your father when you were growing up? How do you think that relationship influenced what you believe about yourself and how you behave?

_____

_____

4. What is a success you listed when working through the *In-Session Activity*? What did you have to overcome to achieve that success? What did you learn in the process?

_____

_____

5. What is one truth about God you have difficulty believing? What is one thing you can do this week to begin renewing your mind when it comes to your false belief about God?

_____

_____

PRIMER:
THE HOMEWORK FOR THIS WEEK
☐ Complete the *False Beliefs vs. Truths* exercise, pp. 40–45. (20 minutes)
☐ Read Session 4, pp. 48–49. (5 minutes)

SECOND COAT:
IF YOU WANT MORE
☐ Complete the *Full History Questionnaire* located in the Appendix, pp. 98–106. (60 minutes)

HOMEWORK:
FALSE BELIEFS VS. TRUTHS

Look back at the false beliefs you checked on pages 15–16 and select the corresponding boxes below. Take some time to read through the opposing truths that relate to the beliefs you selected. Next time the false belief crops up, see if you can focus your mind around the truth instead of giving that false belief power over your thoughts and actions.

FALSE BELIEF	TRUTH
☐ 1. I must be in control to be safe, secure, or significant.	I do not need to be in control because God is in control. Many are the plans in a person's mind, but it is the Lord's purpose that prevails. Proverbs 19:21
☐ 2. I must please other people to be loved or accepted.	I am to please God, rather than seek the approval of people. Am I now trying to win the approval of human beings, or of God? Or am I trying to please people? If I were still trying to please people, I would not be a servant of Christ. Galatians 1:10
☐ 3. I must overcome and make it; I must be tough and independent to survive.	I am dependent on God. Apart from him, I can do nothing. I [Jesus] am the vine; you are the branches. If you remain in me and I in you, you will bear much fruit; apart from me you can do nothing. John 15:5
☐ 4. To be safe and secure, I must be guarded and not risk intimacy.	Christ's peace will guard my heart and mind. And the peace of God, which transcends all understanding, will guard your hearts and your minds in Christ Jesus. Philippians 4:7
☐ 5. Emotions always represent truth.	Emotions can and will deceive me. The heart is deceitful above all things and beyond cure. Who can understand it? Jeremiah 17:9

Material adapted from *Old Beliefs vs New Beliefs* by Anne Trippe. Used with permission.

FALSE BELIEF	TRUTH
☐ 6. For me to be content, life must be fair.	I can learn to be content in my circumstances through Christ. I am not saying this because I am in need, for I have learned to be content whatever the circumstances. Philippians 4:11
☐ 7. I am unworthy of love or acceptance.	Nothing can separate me from the love of God in Christ. For I am convinced that… [nothing] will be able to separate us from the love of God that is in Christ Jesus our Lord. Romans 8:38–39
☐ 8. I must be right to be significant or to know I am of value.	My value and significance come from a humble dependence on God. God opposes the proud but shows favor to the humble. 1 Peter 5:5
☐ 9. I must be heard to know I am of value.	My value comes from God, not other people. God opposes the proud but shows favor to the humble. 1 Peter 5:5
☐ 10. I cannot be okay or at peace if those around me are not okay.	My peace comes from the Lord, not other people. Peace I [Jesus] leave with you; my peace I give you. John 14:27
☐ 11. I deserve special treatment from other people.	I am called to value others above myself. In humility value others above yourselves, not looking to your own interests but each of you to the interests of the others. Philippians 2:3–4
☐ 12. I must have respect to know I am of value.	True respect and honor come from God, not other people. Wealth and honor come from [God; he is] the ruler of all things. 1 Chronicles 29:12
☐ 13. I must perform/achieve to be accepted.	God accepts me—not because of anything I have done. [God] saved us, not because of righteous things we had done, but because of his mercy. Titus 3:5

FALSE BELIEF	TRUTH
☐ 14. What I do makes me who I am.	What I do does not define who I am. [God] saved us, not because of righteous things we had done, but because of his mercy. Titus 3:5
☐ 15. My loved ones must change for me to be content and at peace.	Peace and contentment come from God. Do not be anxious about anything, but… present your requests to God. And the peace of God, which transcends all understanding, will guard your hearts and your minds in Christ Jesus. Philippians 4:6–7
☐ 16. Other people must meet my needs.	God is the ultimate source of provision for all my needs. And my God will meet all your needs according to the riches of his glory in Christ Jesus. Philippians 4:19
☐ 17. I must get revenge on those who have wronged me.	Do not repay evil with evil. Do not repay anyone evil for evil… live at peace with everyone. Romans 12:17–18
☐ 18. I must be protected to know I am safe and secure.	The Lord is my safety and refuge. The Lord is my rock, my fortress and my deliverer; my God is my rock, in whom I take refuge. Psalm 18:2
☐ 19. I must have the approval of other people to know I am of value. Their opinions of me determine my worth.	My approval comes from God, not from pleasing people. Am I now trying to win the approval of human beings, or of God? Or am I trying to please people? If I were still trying to please people, I would not be a servant of Christ. Galatians 1:10
☐ 20. I must be in a relationship or married to be satisfied, secure, or significant.	Only God, not a relationship, will ultimately meet my needs. And my God will meet all your needs according to the riches of his glory in Christ Jesus. Philippians 4:19
☐ 21. If I follow the Lord, life will be hard.	Trouble happens to everyone. I have told you these things, so that in me you may have peace. In this world you will have trouble. But take heart! I have overcome the world. John 16:33
☐ 22. I am a victim.	I'm a conqueror, not a victim. In all these things we are more than conquerors through [Christ] who loved us. Romans 8:37

FALSE BELIEF	TRUTH
☐ 23. My past determines who I am.	My past is not who I am. I am new. If anyone is in Christ, the new creation has come: The old has gone, the new is here! 2 Corinthians 5:17
☐ 24. I must meet certain standards to love, accept, and feel good about myself.	God loves me not based on what I do, but because of his mercy. When the kindness and love of God our Savior appeared, he saved us, not because of the righteous things we had done, but because of his mercy. Romans 5:8
☐ 25. I must have a child to fill my emptiness.	Only God, not a child, promises to fulfill me. And my God will meet all your needs according to the riches of his glory in Christ Jesus. Philippians 4:19
☐ 26. I must figure out my future to be secure.	My future is secured by God. Consider the ravens: They do not sow or reap… yet God feeds them; [so consider] how much more valuable you are than the birds. Luke 12:24
☐ 27. I can't handle this.	I can do all things through Christ. I can do all this through him who gives me strength. Philippians 4:13
☐ 28. I must be appreciated to know I am of value.	God sees what I do, regardless of appreciation from other people. She gave this name to the Lord who spoke to her: "You are the God who sees me." Colossians 3:32
☐ 29. I do not measure up.	Because of Jesus, I am enough. For by one sacrifice [Jesus] has made perfect forever those who are being made holy. Hebrews 10:14
☐ 30. I'm worthless. I will never amount to anything.	I was valuable before I was born. I am fearfully and wonderfully made. Psalm 139:14
☐ 31. I am responsible for the happiness of other people, and they are responsible for mine.	I am not responsible for the happiness of other people. God is. May the God of hope fill you with all joy and peace… so that you may overflow with hope. Romans 15:13

FALSE BELIEF	TRUTH
☐ 32. I must fix problems to know I am secure.	I must be still and wait for the Lord to rescue me. I waited patiently for the Lord; he turned to me and heard my cry. . . he set my feet on a rock and gave me a firm place to stand. Psalm 40:1–2
☐ 33. In order to feel worthy, I must not fail.	My weakness becomes strength by the power of Jesus. But he said to me, "My grace is sufficient for you, for my power is made perfect in weakness." 2 Corinthians 12:9
☐ 34. I must be the best to know that I am of value.	I am to value others above myself. In humility value others above yourselves, not looking to your own interests but each of you to the interests of the others. Philippians 2:3–4
☐ 35. I must get my way to be satisfied and content.	My satisfaction comes from God. For [God's] thoughts are not your thoughts, neither are your ways [God's] ways. Isaiah 55:8
☐ 36. I must earn love.	I am already loved by God. God demonstrates his own love for us in this: While we were still sinners, Christ died for us. Romans 5:8
☐ 37. Real men do not show they need help.	Pride is followed by destruction. Pride goes before destruction, a haughty spirit before a fall. Proverbs 16:18
☐ 38. I cannot be happy unless my circumstances change.	I can be content in my circumstances through Christ who strengthens me. I am not saying this because I am in need, for I have learned to be content whatever the circumstances. Philippians 4:11
☐ 39. I must be understood to have peace and contentment.	I am known and understood by God. You have searched me, Lord, and you know me. You know when I sit down and when I rise. Psalm 139:1–2

FALSE BELIEF	TRUTH
☐ 40. I cannot allow other people to see my flaws. I must be perfect to know I am of value and to be secure.	Christ's power is made perfect in my weakness. But he said to me, "My grace is sufficient for you, for my power is made perfect in weakness." 2 Corinthians 12:9
☐ 41. The shame of my past is my fault, and I am to blame for the consequences of it.	I am no longer condemned. Therefore, there is now no condemnation for those who are in Christ Jesus. Romans 8:1
☐ 42. I am who I am. I shouldn't have to change.	God's plan for me is to mature and grow. Speaking the truth in love, we will grow to become in every respect the mature body of [Jesus] who is the head. Ephesians 4:11
☐ 43. I deserve what I have. I worked hard for it.	I am entitled to nothing. It is given as a gift. Every good and perfect gift is from above, coming down from the Father. James 1:17
☐ 44. I must prove myself to know my worth.	I am valuable regardless of my works or successes. For it is by grace you have been saved… it is the gift of God—not by works, so that no one can boast. Ephesians 2:8–9
☐ 45. I must take care of myself.	God will take care of me. The Lord is my strength and my defense; he has become my salvation. Psalm 118:14
☐ 46. Others cannot be trusted.	I can trust God, even when I cannot trust people. Trust in the Lord with all your heart and lean not on your own understanding; in all your ways submit to him, and he will make your paths straight. Proverbs 3:5–6
☐ 47. I must protect my reputation to feel valued.	I can trust God with my reputation. I don't need to fear what people think. Fear of man will prove to be a snare, but whoever trusts in the Lord is kept safe. Proverbs 29:25

4

Call a Professional

SESSION 4:
CALL A PROFESSIONAL

We spend money on books, counselors, doctors, and conferences trying to fix ourselves. People have been plagued by sin and struggles since the beginning of time. Some people lose marriages, jobs, relationships, and homes—all because they tried too hard to solve problems they weren't capable of solving.

Nearly two thousand years ago, the apostle Paul, who wrote most of the New Testament, diagnosed what's wrong with us. In a letter to the Christian church in Rome, he wrote:

> For I have the desire to do what is good, but I cannot carry it out. For I do not do the good I want to do, but the evil I do not want to do—this I keep on doing. (Romans 7:18–19)

You've experienced something similar, right? You want to live according to a certain set of standards. It could have something to do with honesty or how you treat others. It's easy to hold others to those standards. But you do not always maintain them yourself. You find yourself yelling at your kids, criticizing your spouse, or keeping the money when the cashier at the grocery store gives you too much change.

Many people don't know what the problem is, yet they try to fix it anyway. It's like looking under your car's hood when you don't know anything about cars; it might make you feel like you're doing something useful, but you still won't be able to fix the car. You can't solve a problem if you don't know what's wrong.

FREEDOM IN CHRIST

So, where do we solve the problem of knowing what we should do but not being able to do it? Start with the truth that being a Christian means you are in Christ. Jesus' death on the cross paid for your sins and changed your identity by placing you in God's family. You're given Jesus' past, present, and future. When he died on the cross, you died with him. When God raised him from the dead, he raised you too. In Galatians 2:20, the apostle Paul explains it this way:

> I have been crucified in Christ and I no longer live, but Christ lives in me. The life I now live in the body, I live by faith in the Son of God, who loved me and gave himself for me.

Christ's death and resurrection demonstrated his power over sin. We have that power too. That's so freeing!

> For we know that our old self was crucified in him so that the body ruled by sin might be done away with, that we should no longer be slaves to sin. (Romans 6:6)

If this is true, why do we continue to say yes to a master that is no longer our master? Christ has given us the freedom of a new life, one in which we have the power to say no to sin. Some of us have said yes to sin our entire lives because we didn't know that Jesus had given us mastery over it. Sin may taunt and tempt us, but our new way of life is Jesus reigning in us.

CONCLUSION

We all wonder why we do things that hurt us and why we can't break bad habits. We look for solutions in books or sermons. We look for a *what* that will rescue us.

> What a wretched man I am! Who will rescue me from this body that is subject to death? (Romans 7:24)

The truth is that the solution to our problem isn't a book or a sermon. It's not discipline or willpower. It's not a *what* at all. It's a *who*.

VIDEO NOTES

SESSION 4 COMMUNICATOR: CLAY SCROGGINS

Clay is the lead pastor of North Point Community Church. In this role, Clay provides visionary and directional leadership for the local church staff and congregation. Clay has been married to his wife, Jenny, for eight years, and they have four children.

DISCUSSION QUESTIONS

1. In what ways do you think our culture's definition of "freedom" is inadequate? What are some potential costs of misunderstanding something as important as freedom?

2. During the video message, Clay says that we're only free when we depend on God. Do you think it's possible to be free and dependent at the same time? Why or why not?

3. Over the past three sessions, you explored the connection between false beliefs and unhealthy behaviors. Talk about how some of your false beliefs have stolen your freedom.

4. Read Proverbs 29:25. How do you think concern about what other people think about you may be preventing you from reaching your full potential?

> Fear of man will prove to be a snare, but whoever trusts in the Lord is kept safe. (Proverbs 29:25)

5. Look back at the needs—security, satisfaction, and significance—that you explored in the *In-Session Activity* on pages 21–23. What is one thing you can do this week to start depending on Jesus to meet those needs? (Use the *Freedom Exercise* on pages 53 and 54 to explore this topic in greater depth.)

PRIMER:
THE HOMEWORK FOR THIS WEEK
☐ Complete the *Freedom Exercise*, pp. 53–54. (15 minutes)
☐ Read Session 5, p. 56. (5 minutes)

SECOND COAT:
IF YOU WANT MORE
☐ After completing the *Freedom Exercise*, spend some additional time reading your answers and thinking about the content from this session.

HOMEWORK:
FREEDOM EXERCISE

When we become Christians, we become new creations. This exercise is designed to help you discover what it means to be a "new creation" and how to move toward the freedom that is offered to you.

1. People who claim to be Christians tend to fall into one of the three categories listed below. Circle the category that you most identify with.

   1. They believe what Jesus has done for them, and they live in freedom knowing they have a new identity and power in Christ.

   2. They believe what Jesus has done for them, but they still live controlled by false beliefs in different areas of their lives.

   3. They do not believe what Jesus has done for them, and they live outside the freedom offered in Christ.

2. On pages 21–23, you completed an assessment of your needs. Refer back to those pages now. Pick one or two areas you believe are controlling how you have acted and felt this week, and list those areas below.

_____

_____

_____

_____

3. Which false belief is fueling the needs you listed in question two?
   (See pages 40–45 for examples of false beliefs.)

   _____

   _____

   _____

4. Based on the answers to questions two and three, set a goal to start each
   day this week with a prayer similar to the sample below:

   Jesus,
   *I am tired of seeking **satisfaction and value (need)** from **my job**. I need help*
   living in the power and freedom of who you say I am. I have been believing that
   ***my job determines my worth (false belief)**, and this is not true. I want to choose,*
   *this week, to believe that **I am valuable regardless of what I do (truth)**.*

   Jesus,

   I'm tired of seeking _____ from _____ .
                   (security, satisfaction, or significance)   (e.g., my career)

   I need help living in the power and freedom of who you say I am. I have been

   believing that _____ , and this is not true. I want
                 (your false belief)

   to choose this week to believe that _____ .
                               (the truth)

   We are offered freedom in Christ. When you find yourself drifting toward
   a false belief or unhealthy behavior, you can pray and ask God for help.
   The more you start to focus on God instead of your belief or behaviors,
   the more you will discover the freedom that is possible through a deep
   dependence on Christ.

5

Draw Up the Plan

SESSION 5:
DRAW UP THE PLAN

When you were little, people probably asked you, "What do you want to be when you grow up?" What they were really asking is, "What do you want to do?"

We spend much of our lives creating labels for ourselves in an effort to define who we are. What if God created you with an altogether different identity in mind?

IDENTITY IN CHRIST

When you became a Christian, you gained a new identity. You became a new creation in Christ, and a child of God. In 2 Corinthians 5:17, Paul says, "Therefore, if anyone is in Christ, the new creation has come: The old has gone, the new is here."

Knowing your new identity doesn't mean you won't still be tempted to return to your old way of thinking and your old identity. If you continue to identify with who you used to be and how you used to act, you will continue to live the way you used to live.

CONCLUSION

How do you know if you are finding your identity in something or someone? Ask yourself:

"Would I be devastated if I lost it?"

"Do I want it more than I want God?"

Too many Christians don't know who they are in Christ and continually struggle to find their value in relationships, possessions, and accomplishments. As you read the Bible, you will discover the offer of a new identity. This new identity, however, is challenging to accept because it goes against what culture tells you to believe about yourself. In Christ, a new identity is available that is strong, clear, and unchanging.

Video Notes

SESSION 5 COMMUNICATOR: RODNEY ANDERSON

Rodney has been in ministry for over 15 years, working with both students and adults. He has been on staff with Buckhead Church for five years and is currently serving as the Singles Multi-Campus Director. He loves good food and Georgia football. Rodney and his wife, Sarah, have two amazing boys.

DISCUSSION QUESTIONS

(Part 1)

1. Complete the following sentence: *I am* _____.
   Why do you think you define yourself that way?

   _____

   _____

2. During the video, Rodney says we were created to have God tell us we're
   valuable. Do you agree? Why or why not?

   _____

   _____

3. What thing or person do you believe you couldn't live without? When you think
   about prioritizing God above that thing or person, which emotions are stirred
   in you?

   _____

   _____

Following *Discussion Questions* 1–3, complete the following *In-Session Activity*.

IN-SESSION ACTIVITY

Below is a list of truths about your new identity in Christ. Give each statement below a 1, 2, 3, or 4 using these definitions:

1 = I do not believe this.
2 = I struggle to believe this.
3 = I believe this in my head.
4 = I believe this in my head and my heart.

IN CHRIST...

	Statement	Scripture
☐	I am part of God's family.	To those who believed in his name, he gave the right to become children of God. John 1:12
☐	I belong to God.	You were bought at a price. 1 Corinthians 6:20
☐	I am chosen by God.	For he chose us ... before the creation of the world. Ephesians 1:4
☐	I am forgiven.	In [Jesus] we have . . . the forgiveness of sins. Ephesians 1:7
☐	I am blameless.	There is now no condemnation for those who are in Christ Jesus. Romans 8:1
☐	I am not condemned.	For he chose us . . . to be blameless in his sight. Ephesians 1:4
☐	I am included.	You also were included in Christ when you heard the message of truth. Ephesians 1:13
☐	I am righteous and holy.	But you are a chosen people . . . a holy nation, God's special possession. 2 Peter 2:9

IN CHRIST...

☐	I am near to God.	You who were once far away have been brought near by the blood of Christ. Ephesians 2:13
☐	I am safe.	[Jesus] keeps them safe, and the evil one cannot harm them. 1 John 5:18
☐	I am new.	If anyone is in Christ . . . the old has gone, the new is here! 2 Corinthians 5:17
☐	I can't be separated from God's love.	Neither height nor depth, nor anything else in all creation, will be able to separate us from the love of God. Romans 8:39
☐	I am protected.	The name of the LORD is a fortified tower; the righteous run to it and are safe. Proverbs 18:10
☐	I belong to the light, not the darkness.	You are all children of the light . . . We do not belong to the night or to the darkness. 1 Thessalonians 5:5
☐	I have everything I need.	Consider the ravens: They do not sow or reap . . . yet God feeds them [so consider] how much more valuable you are than the birds. Luke 12:24
☐	I am a citizen of heaven.	They were longing for a better country—a heavenly one. Therefore God is not ashamed to be called their God, for he has prepared a city for them. Hebrews 11:16
☐	I am a stranger to this world.	Dear friends, I urge you, as foreigners and exiles, to abstain from sinful desires, which wage war against your soul. 1 Peter 2:11
☐	I am secure.	You are no longer foreigners and strangers, but fellow… members of [God's] household, with Christ Jesus as the chief cornerstone. Ephesians 2:19–20
☐	I house the Holy Spirit within me.	Don't you know that you yourselves are God's temple and that God's Spirit dwells in your midst? 1 Corinthians 3:16
☐	I am not alone.	God has said, "Never will I leave you." Hebrews 13:5

IN CHRIST...

☐	I have the mind of Christ.	We have the mind of Christ. 1 Corinthians 2:16
☐	I am greatly loved.	[You are] God's chosen people, holy and dearly loved. Colossians 3:12
☐	I am free from the power of sin.	Our old self was crucified with [Jesus] so that… we should no longer be slaves to sin. Romans 6:6
☐	I am connected to Jesus.	I [Jesus] am the vine; you are the branches… remain in me and I in you. John 15:5
☐	I am a friend of Jesus.	I [Jesus] no longer call you servants…Instead I have called you friends. John 15:15
☐	I am complete in Jesus.	For in Christ all the fullness of the Deity lives in bodily form, and in Christ you have been brought to fullness (*completeness*). Colossians 2:9–10
☐	I do not need to be in control because God is in control.	Many are the plans in a person's mind, but it is the Lord's purpose that prevails. Proverbs 19:21

Once you have completed the activity, continue the *Discussion Questions* on the following page.

DISCUSSION QUESTIONS

(Part 2)

4. What trends emerged as you worked through the *In-Session Activity*? (Are there statements you struggle to believe? Is it common for you to believe statements in your head but not in your heart?)

_____

_____

5. Pick one of the "In Christ..." statements you struggle to believe. What is one thing you can do this week to surrender that truth to Christ? How can this group support you?

_____

_____

PRIMER:
THE HOMEWORK FOR THIS WEEK
☐ Read Session 6, pp. 64–65. (5 minutes)

SECOND COAT:
IF YOU WANT MORE
☐ Spend some additional time reading your *In Christ* activity, pp. 59–61. Think about the content from this session.

6

Demo Day

SESSION 6:
DEMO DAY

Why do we have to suffer and go through trials? If God is good, shouldn't life be good all the time? Even if suffering is necessary for some people, why do Christians have to experience it? Shouldn't we, as God's children, get free passes? Sometimes it feels like non-Christians get the free passes to avoid suffering.

If we're talking about renovating our lives, suffering is often God's form of demolition. It's a way of clearing out our old ways of believing, behaving, and feeling in order to make way for something new and better.

Suffering is necessary because it can lead us to brokenness—complete surrender of everything we rely on for our identities, except Christ. Brokenness isn't a condition but a position or attitude. It is when God brings us to the end of ourselves. It's where we want nothing more than him. Through our brokenness, God redeems our suffering so we can experience abundant life.

GOD'S PURPOSE FOR BROKENNESS

God's ultimate purpose for brokenness is to break our dependency on anything other than him. It's to make us aware of our complete dependence on him. He doesn't want us to suffer. He's not trying to punish us. He knows that the only way we can experience abundant life is to depend solely and completely on him—and he loves us deeply enough to allow trials and suffering to make us aware of that dependence.

It's not necessary for us to know or understand the purposes of our circumstances. In fact, sometimes we pray for God to change our circumstances when he is actually using those circumstances to accomplish his purposes.

CONCLUSION

Difficult circumstances help us grow and rely on God. He wants to minister to others through us. Every trial we face brings an awareness of our own insufficiency and an increased dependence upon his complete sufficiency.

VIDEO NOTES

SESSION 6 COMMUNICATOR: ANDY JONES

Andy is the Middle School (Transit) Director at Woodstock City Church. In this role, he leads the Transit staff and oversees a department with over 150 volunteers and more than 500 middle school students. Andy graduated from Liberty University. He and his wife, Christina, have two children, Eli and Peyton.

DISCUSSION QUESTIONS

1. Have you ever seen someone grow as a result of suffering? If so, how did the experience change your perception of that person?

2. Why do you think we're tempted to believe that suffering is abnormal and a pain-free life is possible? What are some of the costs of that false belief?

3. How do you tend to respond to suffering? Do you try to deflect it, numb it, run from it, or face it head-on? What is the downside to that tendency?

4. On page 64, we read that "God's ultimate purpose for brokenness is to break our dependence on anything other than him." Does this seem fair? Why or why not?

5. What is one area of your life in which you need to surrender your will to God? What is one thing you can do this week to surrender? How can this group support you?

_____

_____

PRIMER:
THE HOMEWORK FOR THIS WEEK
☐ Complete the *Letting Go* exercise, pp. 69–70. (15 minutes)
☐ Read Session 7, pp. 72–73. (5 minutes)

SECOND COAT:
IF YOU WANT MORE
☐ After completing the *Letting Go* exercise, spend some additional time reading your answers and thinking about the content from this session.

HOMEWORK:
LETTING GO

Below is a list of things we try to hold onto or depend on other than Christ. Read through the list and select the statements that are true for you.

I STRUGGLE TO LET GO OF MY RIGHT...

☐ To my opinions

☐ To my timing

☐ To the fulfillments of my expectations

☐ To judge

☐ To be loved

☐ To be thanked or appreciated

☐ To be married

☐ To have a child

☐ To blame

☐ To rescue

☐ To be rescued

☐ To be needed or wanted

☐ To have the approval of other people

☐ To be heard

☐ To take offense

☐ To be justified

☐ To have an attractive body

☐ To have wealth

☐ To my time

☐ To life itself

☐ To my life looking like it did in the past

☐ To my habits

☐ To my future plans and dreams

☐ To control, fix, or direct

☐ To be significant

☐ To prosper

☐ To know future outcomes

☐ To get my way

☐ To success

☐ To my choices

☐ To my occupation

☐ To be used by God

☐ To escape or avoid bad circumstances

☐ To fear

☐ To be emotionally secure

☐ To experience pleasant circumstances

☐ To be accepted

☐ To be understood

☐ To be acknowledged

☐ To have relationships

☐ To have a happy marriage

☐ To tell others what I know

☐ To meet the needs of other people

☐ To financial success

☐ To be right

☐ To defend

☐ To have justice done

☐ To be happy

☐ To be healthy

☐ To my possessions

☐ To be comfortable

☐ To my recreation time or activities

☐ To my geographical location

☐ To self-sufficiency

☐ To my satisfaction

☐ To my securities

☐ To be strong

☐ To my reputation

☐ To my feelings

☐ To notoriety

☐ To know God's will

☐ To demand things from God

God does not promise any of these things. We often think that we deserve or have earned them. When you let go of your rights and become fully surrendered, God is able to do unbelievable things … more than you could ever imagine.

7

Take Out the Trash

SESSION 7:
TAKE OUT THE TRASH

We're all familiar with the word "forgiveness." We first hear it when we're small children, and we are regularly reminded of it until we reach old age. Few people really understand what it means. We like forgiveness when we receive it from others or when we associate it with Jesus' death on the cross. Alternatively, when we are the ones forgiving, it makes us uncomfortable… maybe even depressed, resentful, or nauseated. Refusing to forgive can even affect our physical health because God didn't create our bodies as harbors of grievance and resentment. Forgiveness is just as much for us as it is for the people we forgive. In fact, it is *more* for us than for them.

Opportunities to forgive tend to be coupled with intense emotions. Someone has wronged us. Anger, hurt, or bitterness can deceive us into thinking that forgiveness isn't possible until our emotions have healed. The truth is that the ability to forgive isn't dependent on the state of our emotions.

WHAT FORGIVENESS IS AND ISN'T

Forgiveness is not…

Forgiveness ≠ A feeling or emotion

Forgiveness ≠ Excusing the other person's behavior

Forgiveness ≠ Forgetting

Forgiveness ≠ Reconciliation

Forgiveness is...

Forgiveness is a choice you make, through faith in God, to give up the right to hold another person accountable for the wrong done to you. That doesn't mean you won't grieve what you've lost as a result of the wrong. Grieving is important. Healing continues beyond the moment you choose to forgive.

CONCLUSION

When we think about forgiveness, we tend to focus on our relationships with other people. When we do so, forgiveness may not seem worth the effort because those relationships often can't be restored even when we forgive. But forgiveness has a greater purpose: the restoration of our relationship with Christ. A lack of forgiveness can be one of the biggest hindrances to living fully free in Christ. When we refuse to forgive, it becomes toxic to us, changes our behavior, and causes us to hold Jesus at arm's length.

VIDEO NOTES

SESSION 7 COMMUNICATOR: ELAINE SCOTT

Elaine is the Director of Women's Groups at Browns Bridge Church. In her role, she provides pastoral and strategic leadership to the women's community. She is also a member of the Leadership Team at Browns Bridge, a group entrusted with providing vision and direction for the church. She is married and has two children.

DISCUSSION QUESTIONS

1. Talk about a time when someone forgave you for something you'd done, large or small. What did that person's forgiveness do for you? What do you think it did for him or her?

_____

_____

2. Read Matthew 5:44. Is the idea of loving your enemies and praying for those who persecute you challenging for you? Why or why not?

> But I tell you, love your enemies and pray for those who persecute you. (Matthew 5:44)

_____

_____

3. In the video, Elaine defines "forgiveness" as "a choice you make, through faith in God, to give up the right to hold another person accountable for the wrong done to you." Do you agree with that definition? Why or why not?

_____

_____

4. Do you think it's possible to forgive someone who continues to do things that hurt you? Why or why not?

_____

_____

5. Is there someone in your life or from your past that you need to forgive? What can you do to take a step toward forgiveness? How can this group support you?

_____

_____

PRIMER:
THE HOMEWORK FOR THIS WEEK
☐ Read Session 8, pp. 82–83. (5 minutes)

SECOND COAT:
IF YOU WANT MORE
☐ Complete the *Forgiveness Exercise*, pp. 77–79. (30 minutes)

FORGIVENESS EXERCISE

This exercise will take some time, and it may stir up weighty emotions. Take your time and know that this work will have a lasting impact on your physical, emotional, and spiritual health.

If you would like to revisit this exercise in the future, additional copies are located in the Appendix.

1. Take some time to pray, asking God to reveal to you if anyone has offended you or hurt you. As people come to mind, write their names below.

_____

_____

_____

_____

2. Beside the name(s) you listed, write the offense or hurt you experienced.

3. Write down something you believe about yourself as a result of the hurt you experienced (e.g., my value is dependent on how well I perform).

_____

_____

_____

_____

4. Determine what you lost from the offense you experienced (e.g., a happy childhood, my time).

   Note: This is a hard step in this process. Acknowledging the cost is often one of the most painful parts of the forgiveness journey.

   _____

   _____

   _____

   _____

   _____

   _____

   _____

   _____

   _____

5. Take time to acknowledge the pain each person caused you. Give yourself permission to feel hurt, angry, or sad. Forgiveness is a choice of the will, and you will still grieve. Grieving is important. There is healing that will continue beyond the choice of forgiveness.

6. To forgive, declare that they owe you nothing further, releasing the right to see them change, and accepting them as they are. It is okay to ask God for help with this process. We often can't forgive people through our own efforts and need God to help us truly forgive those that have hurt us. If it helps you, write out your forgiveness declaration in the space provided.

_____

_____

_____

_____

_____

_____

7. When you are finished with the exercise, tear up or burn your list. This represents how you're choosing not to hold people accountable for what they owe you.

No one deserves forgiveness. But God chose to forgive us, and forgiveness is something we can offer, even when people don't deserve it. By identifying specifically how someone has hurt us, we can pinpoint exactly what we are forgiving. Forgiveness is the door we must walk through in order to experience true peace and freedom.

8

Hard Hats On

SESSION 8:
HARD HATS ON

What does it look like to live the Christian life day-by-day? It's rare that anyone explains it to us. More often, we're told about theology or doctrine, but given no advice about how to apply what we've learned to our daily lives.

The Christian life is about yielding ourselves each moment to the source of life: Jesus. That's what Jesus meant when he urged his disciples (and us) to "abide" in him.

> Abide in me, and I in you. As the branch cannot bear fruit by itself, unless it abides in the vine, neither can you, unless you abide in me. (John 15:4)

HOW DO WE ABIDE IN CHRIST?

The dictionary's definition of abiding is *the act of resting in, dwelling in, or depending on.* But abiding in Christ isn't passive. It doesn't mean you do nothing.

When Jesus says to abide in him, he's urging us to stay close to him, to exist in an uninterrupted relationship with him. Jesus called us to abide, but abiding isn't about our own efforts. So, how do we abide in Christ? How do we know when we're successful?

As you abide in Christ, you'll recognize the freedom and abundance of life he produces in and through you—not through your efforts. You'll become more patient, loving toward others, joyful in difficult circumstances, and at peace in scary times—and you'll know you don't deserve credit for these changes in yourself. So, how do you do this? You adopt the attitude of "I can't, but he can through me."

"I can't keep from gossiping, but Jesus can through me."

"I can't control my language during rush-hour traffic, but Jesus can through me."

"I can't honor my parents after everything they've done, but Jesus can through me."

"I can't forgive, but Jesus can through me."

CONCLUSION

You have a choice each day to abide in Christ or to live by the flesh. You can put all of your effort into meeting your needs by whatever means necessary. Or you can trust your heavenly Father to meet your needs. You can abide in Christ, allowing him to express his power through you, conquering sin in your life.

VIDEO NOTES

SESSION 8 COMMUNICATOR: BILLY PHENIX

Billy Phenix has been the lead pastor of Buckhead Church since 2011. In this role, Billy leads the church staff and oversees all aspects of its operations. Before becoming lead pastor, he served in several areas for North Point Ministries, including children's, student, and singles ministries. Billy and his wife, Joy, have two children, Ellie and Josh, as well as a big, yellow Labrador named Mack.

DISCUSSION QUESTIONS

(Part 1)

1. Talk about a time you felt closely connected to God. What was going on in your life at that time? How did your circumstances influence the closeness of your connection to your heavenly Father?

_____

_____

2. We tend to think of reading the Bible and praying as *the* ways we connect with God. What are some other ways people connect with God?

_____

_____

3. What are some things that prevent you from connecting with God?

_____

_____

Following *Discussion Questions* 1–2, complete the following *In-Session Activity*.

IN-SESSION ACTIVITY

As you abide in Christ, you'll recognize the freedom and abundance of life he produces in and through you. Below is a list of words or phrases that describe the behaviors and emotions that characterize a person abiding in Christ.

Check the boxes of the behaviors and emotions that you would like to see more present in your life.

I WANT TO BE A PERSON WHO IS MORE ...

☐ Accepting of others

☐ Accepting of myself

☐ Affirming of other people

☐ Believing of truth

☐ Calm

☐ Clear-minded

☐ Compassionate

☐ Confident in the Lord

☐ Content

☐ Cooperative

☐ Courageous

☐ Dependent on God

☐ Disciplined

☐ Emotionally engaged

☐ Empathetic

☐ Faithful

☐ Forgiving

☐ Free

☐ Generous

☐ Gentle

☐ Gracious

☐ Happy

☐ Honest

☐ Hopeful

☐ Humble

☐ Joyful

☐ Kind

☐ Light-hearted

☐ Loves other people without condition

☐ Merciful

☐ Obedient

☐ Patient

☐ Peaceful

☐ Pure

☐ Quick to listen

☐ Quiet

- ☐ Reasonable
- ☐ Reliable
- ☐ Satisfied
- ☐ Secure
- ☐ Self-controlled
- ☐ Selfless
- ☐ Serving of other people
- ☐ Significant in Christ
- ☐ Slow to speak
- ☐ Social

- ☐ Submissive to authority
- ☐ Surrendered
- ☐ Sympathetic
- ☐ Teachable
- ☐ Thankful
- ☐ Tolerant
- ☐ Transparent
- ☐ Trusting
- ☐ Vocal
- ☐ Vulnerable

Once you have completed the activity, continue the *Discussion Questions* on the following page.

DISCUSSION QUESTIONS

(Part 2)

4. Read Galatians 5:22–23. What similarities, if any, exist between the fruit of the Spirit and the behaviors and emotions you selected in the *In-Session Activity*? What are some things that stand in the way of you being the kind of person you indicated in the activity?

> But the fruit of the Spirit is love, joy, peace, forbearance, kindness, goodness, faithfulness, gentleness and self-control. Against such things there is no law. (Galatians 5:22–23)

5. What is one thing you can do to abide in Christ this week? What can this group do to help you?

PRIMER:
THE HOMEWORK FOR THIS WEEK
☐ Complete the *Summary Exercise*, pp. 89–90. (30 minutes)

SECOND COAT:
IF YOU WANT MORE
☐ Continue your renovation journey beyond the sessions of this study by processing your story and beliefs in light of all that you have learned. Additional copies of several of the exercises are located in the Appendix for you to use in the days ahead.

HOMEWORK:
SUMMARY EXERCISE

Abiding is never passive. It requires us to seek God to meet all our needs. It requires us to replace our false beliefs with truths and to surrender our wills. This exercise is designed to help you walk through the process of abiding this week.

If you would like to revisit this exercise in the future, additional copies are located in the Appendix.

1. What's going on in my life that is bothering me?

_____

_____

2. How do I feel as a result of that circumstance?

_____

_____

3. Which of my false beliefs was triggered?
   (See pages 15–16 for the *Identifying False Beliefs* exercise.)

_____

_____

4. Which behavior or emotion was triggered by my false belief?
   (See pages 26–27 for the *Behaviors and Emotions* exercise.)

_____

_____

5. What is the new belief or truth that can replace my false belief?
(See pages 40–45 for the *False Beliefs* vs. *Truths* exercise.)

_____

_____

6. Who do I need to forgive?

_____

_____

7. What additional rights do I need to surrender?
(See pages 69–70 for the "Rights" activity.)

_____

_____

8. What is the new behavior or emotion that can replace my old one?
(See pages 86–87 for characteristics of a person who is abiding in Christ.)

_____

_____

_____

Abiding may be difficult at first; it may even seem unnatural. However, abiding can become a habit and your default to handling tough circumstances in your life. More important, abiding can be the daily posture for how you approach life. Abiding is not a one-time decision, nor is it something we only do for a season. The more you abide, the more you will see evidence of God working in your life.

The Project Continues...

You've completed *Renovate!* We hope you've found it helpful. Know that your journey has just begun. Like a home renovation, personal renovation can feel endless. But you *will* make progress (even when it doesn't feel like it).

Don't let the moments of *frustration* overshadow the moments of *inspiration*.

Renovation is "dirty work," but if you choose to do it, you'll be happy in the end. You'll grow. You'll begin to love God and other people more than you thought possible. *That* is the "life more abundant" that Jesus talks about.

The results are worth the effort.

Appendix

INFLUENCES: COMMON BY-PRODUCTS

Influences that occur in our lives often bring with them a set of beliefs, behaviors, and emotions. Often, this occurs in the following way:

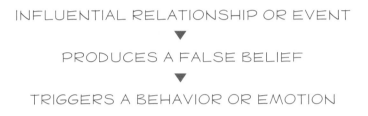

INFLUENTIAL RELATIONSHIP OR EVENT
▼
PRODUCES A FALSE BELIEF
▼
TRIGGERS A BEHAVIOR OR EMOTION

Below is a list (by no means complete) of common, influential relationships and events, followed by common beliefs and behaviors that are often by-products of the listed influences.

Influential Relationships	Possible False Beliefs That Resulted	Possible Behaviors or Emotions That Resulted
Parent who was over-controlling	- I must be in control to feel secure. - I must be the best to validate my worth. - I must show others I am strong and independent.	- Tries to defeat those in authority - Stays emotionally guarded - Likely to be controlling
Parent who was over-indulgent	- Others must do what I want for me to feel loved. - The world must revolve around me for me to be content. - I must receive special treatment to know I am loved.	- Feels entitled to get what he/she wants - Feels rejected if he/she is not indulged or thought of - Possibly spoiled

Influential Relationships	Possible False Beliefs That Resulted	Possible Behaviors or Emotions That Resulted
Parent who was over-protective	- I must rely on a person to feel secure. - I do not measure up. - I am not able to do things on my own.	- Passive - Dependent - Feels inadequate
Parent who was dependent	- I am responsible for the happiness of others and they are responsible for mine. - I must please other people to know I am accepted. - I must be in a relationship to feel secure.	- Has to be in a relationship - Cannot be alone - Only okay if other people are okay
Parent with excessive standards	- I must be perfect to be loved and accepted. - I must please others to avoid rejection. - I must be in control and guarded to feel secure.	- Scared of making mistakes - Follows rules - Pleases and performs for peace and acceptance - May lie to hide imperfections
Parent who gave excessive praise	- I am superior to others. - Words do not mean anything. - If you love me, you will show me.	- Self-absorbed - Self-confident - Self-reliant
Parent who disciplined inconsistently	- I should avoid the consequences of my actions to be content. - Life must be fair for me to be secure or for me to have peace.	- Lacks trust - Not consistent or reliable - Believes life is random and things happen by chance - Feels insecure or unsure
Parent who shamed child	- I do not measure up. - I can't do anything right. - I am inadequate. - Good things will never happen for me.	- Self-condemnation - Believes something is wrong with him/her - Believes he/she cannot do anything right

Influential Relationships	Possible False Beliefs That Resulted	Possible Behaviors or Emotions That Resulted
Parent who denied feelings	- I must be guarded to be safe. - I must be emotionally strong to know I am secure. - I must be strong to know I am safe. - I must be in control to be secure.	- Learns to hide feelings or to not even allow them to exist - Doesn't allow vulnerability - Believes emotions are bad
Parent who expected child to act like a parent	- I am responsible for the well-being of other people. - I must be strong to survive.	- Takes responsibilty for other people's well-being - Controlling
Parent who focused on appearance	- My appearance determines my value. - I am only loved and accepted if I look a certain way.	- Develops an eating disorder - Preoccupation with one's weight and food intake
Parent who minimized problems	- I must avoid conflict to know I am safe. - My problems are not important.	- Becomes someone who takes legitimate problems and says they are not important or things to worry about
Peer rejection	- People are going to reject me. I should just expect it.	- Discouraged about ability or value - Expects others to reject him/her
Peers who shamed	- I am inadequate or unworthy. - I am defective. - Something is wrong with me.	- Self-condemnation or shaming - May avoid situations that could be embarrassing
Peers who were competitive	- I must be the best to know I am of value. - I must be perfect to know I am of value.	- Strives to be the best or the worst - Very competitive

Influential Relationships	Possible False Beliefs That Resulted	Possible Behaviors or Emotions That Resulted
Moved often	- If I get close to others, I am going to get hurt. - To be safe, I must not risk intimacy. - I must be guarded emotionally to be secure.	- Closed off from feelings - Independent or fearful - Adaptable or self-reliant
Abuse (verbal, emotional, physical)	- I am inadequate. - I am unworthy of other people's love. - Something is wrong with me. - Bad things that happen to me are my fault.	- Self-pities or lacks self-worth - Emotionally guarded - Abusive - Angry
Abandonment	- If I get close to others, they will eventually leave me. - People always leave. - I cannot trust others.	- May live in constant fear of abandonment - May not trust other people - May be emotionally guarded
Neglect	- I am forgotten. - I am not important.	- May be uncertain about other people's love - Controlled by doubts

FULL HISTORY QUESTIONNAIRE

Many of the beliefs we have today are a result of the relationships we had with our parents growing up. The following questions will help you look back at your family dynamics and gain a better understanding of who you are today. If a stepparent, family member, or authority figure raised you, also state how he or she influenced you.

1. When you think of your mother, what are a couple of words that come to mind?

_____

_____

_____

2. In what way(s) are you and your mother alike?

_____

_____

_____

3. In what way(s) are you and your mother different?

_____

_____

_____

_____

4. In what way(s) do you wish your mother was different?

_____

_____

_____

5. While you were growing up, how did you spend time with your mother?

_____

_____

_____

6. In what ways, if any, did your mother express love?

_____

_____

_____

7. How do you feel when you are around your mother?

_____

_____

_____

8. What did your mother desire for you to accomplish?

_____

_____

9. When you think of your father, what are a couple of words that come to mind?

_____

_____

_____

10. In what way(s) are you and your father alike?

_____

_____

_____

11. In what way(s) are you and your father different?

_____

_____

_____

12. In what way(s) do you wish your father was different?

_____

_____

_____

13. While you were growing up, how did you spend time with your father?

_____

_____

14. In what ways, if any, did your father express love?

_____

_____

15. How do you feel when you are around your father?

_____

_____

16. What did your father desire for you to accomplish?

_____

_____

17. How many kids were in your family growing up?

_____

_____

18. What was your mother's role or job in your family?

_____

_____

19. What was your father's role or job in your family?

20. What was your role in your family?

21. As a child, how did you get what you wanted?

22. What did discipline look like in your home growing up?

23. As a child, how did you handle conflict or hurt?

24. As a child, how did you deal with fear?

_____

_____

_____

25. When did you feel scared as a child?

_____

_____

_____

26. When did you feel valued as a child?

_____

_____

_____

27. How would you describe your relationships at school growing up?

_____

_____

_____

28. How would you describe your relationships at church growing up?

_____

_____

29. When you think about who are you today, what are some things that frustrate you?

_____

_____

_____

30. What are some things that make you feel happy or content?

_____

_____

_____

31. What is one thing you wish people knew about you?

_____

_____

_____

32. What is one thing you are glad people know about you?

_____

_____

_____

No one has a perfect story. Sometimes what hurts you the most are the people closest to you. These questions can often reveal things about your family that you may have never thought about or perhaps have tried to forget. In order to move forward, you have to deal with your past, but you usually can't do it alone.

Often, people take their answers to these questions and talk through them with a mentor or professional counselor. Inviting a person to discuss your answers will help you gain clarity, hope, and next steps in your story.

FORGIVENESS EXERCISE

(EXTRA COPY OF EXERCISE)

This exercise will take some time, and it may stir up weighty emotions. Take your time and know that this work will have a lasting impact on your physical, emotional, and spiritual health.

1. Take some time to pray, asking God to reveal to you if anyone has offended you or hurt you. As people come to mind, write their names below.

_____

_____

_____

2. Beside the name(s) you listed, write the offense or hurt you experienced.

3. Write down something you believe about yourself as a result of the hurt you experienced (e.g., my value is dependent on how well I perform).

_____

_____

_____

4. Determine what you lost from the offense you experienced (e.g., a happy childhood, my time). Note: This is a hard step in this process. Acknowledging the cost is often one of the most painful parts of the forgiveness journey.

_____

_____

_____

_____

5. Take time to acknowledge the pain each person caused you. Give yourself permission to feel hurt, angry, or sad. Forgiveness is a choice of the will, and you will still grieve. Grieving is important. There is healing that will continue beyond the choice of forgiveness.

6. To forgive, declare that they owe you nothing further, releasing the right to see them change, and accepting them as they are. It is okay to ask God for help with this process. We often can't forgive people through our own efforts and need God to help us truly forgive those that have hurt us. If it helps you, write out your forgiveness declaration in the space provided.

_____

_____

_____

7. When you are finished with the exercise, tear up or burn your list. This represents how you're choosing not to hold people accountable for what they owe you.

_____

No one deserves forgiveness. But God chose to forgive us, and forgiveness is something we can offer, even when people don't deserve it. By identifying specifically how someone has hurt us, we can pinpoint exactly what we are forgiving. Forgiveness is the door we must walk through in order to experience true peace and freedom.

FORGIVENESS EXERCISE

(EXTRA COPY OF EXERCISE)

This exercise will take some time, and it may stir up weighty emotions. Take your time and know that this work will have a lasting impact on your physical, emotional, and spiritual health.

1. Take some time to pray, asking God to reveal to you if anyone has offended you or hurt you. As people come to mind, write their names below.

2. Beside the name(s) you listed, write the offense or hurt you experienced.

3. Write down something you believe about yourself as a result of the hurt you experienced (e.g., my value is dependent on how well I perform).

4. Determine what you lost from the offense you experienced (e.g., a happy childhood, my time). Note: This is a hard step in this process. Acknowledging the cost is often one of the most painful parts of the forgiveness journey.

_____

_____

5. Take time to acknowledge the pain each person caused you. Give yourself permission to feel hurt, angry, or sad. Forgiveness is a choice of the will, and you will still grieve. Grieving is important. There is healing that will continue beyond the choice of forgiveness.

6. To forgive, declare that they owe you nothing further, releasing the right to see them change, and accepting them as they are. It is okay to ask God for help with this process. We often can't forgive people through our own efforts and need God to help us truly forgive those that have hurt us. If it helps you, write out your forgiveness declaration in the space provided.

_____

_____

_____

7. When you are finished with the exercise, tear up or burn your list. This represents how you're choosing not to hold people accountable for what they owe you.

_____

No one deserves forgiveness. But God chose to forgive us, and forgiveness is something we can offer, even when people don't deserve it. By identifying specifically how someone has hurt us, we can pinpoint exactly what we are forgiving. Forgiveness is the door we must walk through in order to experience true peace and freedom.

FORGIVENESS EXERCISE

(EXTRA COPY OF EXERCISE)

This exercise will take some time, and it may stir up weighty emotions. Take your time and know that this work will have a lasting impact on your physical, emotional, and spiritual health.

1. Take some time to pray, asking God to reveal to you if anyone has offended you or hurt you. As people come to mind, write their names below.

2. Beside the name(s) you listed, write the offense or hurt you experienced.

3. Write down something you believe about yourself as a result of the hurt you experienced (e.g., my value is dependent on how well I perform).

4. Determine what you lost from the offense you experienced (e.g., a happy childhood, my time). Note: This is a hard step in this process. Acknowledging the cost is often one of the most painful parts of the forgiveness journey.

_____

_____

5. Take time to acknowledge the pain each person caused you. Give yourself permission to feel hurt, angry, or sad. Forgiveness is a choice of the will, and you will still grieve. Grieving is important. There is healing that will continue beyond the choice of forgiveness.

6. To forgive, declare that they owe you nothing further, releasing the right to see them change, and accepting them as they are. It is okay to ask God for help with this process. We often can't forgive people through our own efforts and need God to help us truly forgive those that have hurt us. If it helps you, write out your forgiveness declaration in the space provided.

_____

_____

_____

7. When you are finished with the exercise, tear up or burn your list. This represents how you're choosing not to hold people accountable for what they owe you.

_____

No one deserves forgiveness. But God chose to forgive us, and forgiveness is something we can offer, even when people don't deserve it. By identifying specifically how someone has hurt us, we can pinpoint exactly what we are forgiving. Forgiveness is the door we must walk through in order to experience true peace and freedom.

SUMMARY EXERCISE

(EXTRA COPY OF EXERCISE)

Abiding is never passive. It requires us to seek God to meet all our needs. It requires us to replace our false beliefs with truths and to surrender our wills. This exercise is designed to help you walk through the process of abiding this week.

1. What's going on in my life that is bothering me?

2. How do I feel as a result of that circumstance?

3. Which of my false beliefs was triggered?
   (See pages 15–16 for the *Identifying False Beliefs* exercise.)

4. Which behavior or emotion was triggered by my false belief?
   (See pages 26–27 for the *Behaviors and Emotions* exercise.)

5. What is the new belief or truth that can replace my false belief?
(See pages 40–45 for the *False Beliefs vs. Truths* exercise.)

_____

_____

6. Who do I need to forgive?

_____

_____

7. What additional rights do I need to surrender?
(See pages 69–70 for the rights activity.)

_____

_____

8. What is the new behavior or emotion that can replace my old one?
(See pages 86–87 for characteristics of a person who is abiding in Christ.)

_____

_____

Abiding may be difficult at first; it may even seem unnatural. However, abiding can become a habit and your default to handling tough circumstances in your life. More importantly, abiding can be the daily posture for how you approach life. Abiding is not a one-time decision, nor is it something we only do for a season. The more you abide, the more you will see evidence of God working in your life.

SUMMARY EXERCISE

(EXTRA COPY OF EXERCISE)

Abiding is never passive. It requires us to seek God to meet all our needs. It requires us to replace our false beliefs with truths and to surrender our wills. This exercise is designed to help you walk through the process of abiding this week.

1. What's going on in my life that is bothering me?

2. How do I feel as a result of that circumstance?

3. Which of my false beliefs was triggered?
   (See pages 15–16 for the *Identifying False Beliefs* exercise.)

4. Which behavior or emotion was triggered by my false belief?
   (See pages 26–27 for the *Behaviors and Emotions* exercise.)

5. What is the new belief or truth that can replace my false belief?
   (See pages 40–45 for the *False Beliefs vs. Truths* exercise.)

   _____

   _____

6. Who do I need to forgive?

   _____

   _____

7. What additional rights do I need to surrender?
   (See pages 69–70 for the rights activity.)

   _____

   _____

8. What is the new behavior or emotion that can replace my old one?
   (See pages 86–87 for characteristics of a person who is abiding in Christ.)

   _____

   _____

Abiding may be difficult at first; it may even seem unnatural. However, abiding can become a habit and your default to handling tough circumstances in your life. More importantly, abiding can be the daily posture for how you approach life. Abiding is not a one-time decision, nor is it something we only do for a season. The more you abide, the more you will see evidence of God working in your life.

SUMMARY EXERCISE

(EXTRA COPY OF EXERCISE)

Abiding is never passive. It requires us to seek God to meet all our needs. It requires us to replace our false beliefs with truths and to surrender our wills. This exercise is designed to help you walk through the process of abiding this week.

1. What's going on in my life that is bothering me?

_____

_____

2. How do I feel as a result of that circumstance?

_____

_____

3. Which of my false beliefs was triggered?
   (See pages 15–16 for the *Identifying False Beliefs* exercise.)

_____

_____

4. Which behavior or emotion was triggered by my false belief?
   (See pages 26–27 for the *Behaviors and Emotions* exercise.)

_____

_____

5. What is the new belief or truth that can replace my false belief?
   (See pages 40–45 for the *False Beliefs vs. Truths* exercise.)

   _____

   _____

6. Who do I need to forgive?

   _____

   _____

7. What additional rights do I need to surrender?
   (See pages 69–70 for the rights activity.)

   _____

   _____

8. What is the new behavior or emotion that can replace my old one?
   (See pages 86–87 for characteristics of a person who is abiding in Christ.)

   _____

   _____

Abiding may be difficult at first; it may even seem unnatural. However, abiding can become a habit and your default to handling tough circumstances in your life. More importantly, abiding can be the daily posture for how you approach life. Abiding is not a one-time decision, nor is it something we only do for a season. The more you abide, the more you will see evidence of God working in your life.

Leader Guide

LEADER GUIDE

LEADER VIDEOS

To coach *Renovate* leaders through each session, **two-minute leader videos** specific to each session are available at **GroupLeaders.org/Renovate**.

DURING A RENOVATE MEETING

SOCIALIZE (10 minutes)
Spend a few minutes getting to know one another and catching up.

DISCUSS (10 minutes – Optional)
Talk about the homework completed the previous week.
Was anything helpful to you? If so, what?
What was more challenging than you expected?

WATCH (15 minutes)
The video session enhances the materials in the workbook by providing additional content on the topic.

DISCUSS (45 minutes)
The Discussion Questions provided in each session help participants explore the topic in conversation with one another. Be patient. The questions are designed to allow participants the freedom to reveal tensions or struggles with the topic, make personal discoveries, or think more about the subject.

REVIEW THE HOMEWORK (5 minutes)
The *Renovate* experience is different for each person. Some people may choose not to complete certain exercises, while others will want to complete all of them. Assure participants that they have the freedom to do as much or as little of the homework as they desire.

PRAY (5 minutes)

Sharing prayer requests and praying for one another is an important part of the *Renovate* experience. It is also okay if a participant doesn't share anything. Never apply pressure for participants to disclose prayer requests.

LEADER – BEFORE EACH RENOVATE MEETING

Read the upcoming session's **materials**. (5 minutes)
Optional – Watch the upcoming video session. (15 minutes)

Review the upcoming session's **exercises**. (5 minutes)
Optional – Complete the upcoming session's exercises. (30 minutes)

Review the upcoming session's **Discussion Questions**. (5 minutes)

FACILITATING THE DISCUSSION

Here are five things to consider when facilitating discussion during your meetings:

Cultivate discussion.

It's easy to assume that a session succeeds or fails based on the quality of your ideas. That's not true. It's the ideas of everyone participating that make a *Renovate* meeting successful. Your role is to create an environment in which people feel safe to share their thoughts.

Point to the material.

Sometimes you'll simply read a discussion question and invite everyone to respond. The conversation will take care of itself. At other times, you may need to encourage participants to share their ideas. Go with the flow, but be ready to nudge the conversation in the right direction when necessary.

Depart from the material.

You don't have to stick rigidly to the Discussion Questions in this workbook. Knowing when to depart from them is more art than science, but no one knows more about your participants than you do.

Stay on track.

This is the flip side to the previous point. While you want to leave space for participants to think through the discussion, make sure the conversation is contributing to the bottom line for the session. Don't let it veer off on tangents. Politely refocus the conversation.

Pray.

This is the most important thing you can do as a leader. Pray for your participants. Pray for your own leadership. Pray that God is not only present at your sessions, but is directing them.